100

things you should know about

SHARKS

100

things you should know about

SHARKS

Steve Parker

Consultant: Trevor Day

Miles Kelly
PUBLISHING

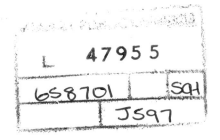
First published in 2005 by
Miles Kelly Publishing Ltd
Bardfield Centre, Great Bardfield, Essex, CM7 4SL

Copyright © Miles Kelly Publishing Ltd 2005

2 4 6 8 10 9 7 5 3 1

Editorial Director: Belinda Gallagher
Assistant Editor: Rosalind McGuire
Designer: Elaine Wilkinson
Picture Researcher: Liberty Newton
Copy Editor: Sarah Ridley
Proofreader: Emma Wild
Indexer: Jane Parker

ISBN 1-84236-537-1

Printed in China

British Library Cataloguing-in-Publication Data
A catalogue record for this book is available from
the British Library

ACKNOWLEDGEMENTS
The publishers would like to thank the following artists who have
contributed to this book:

John Butler Mike Foster Colin Howard Mick Loates
A. Menchi /Studio Galante Andrea Morandi Andy Robinson Rudi Vizi

Cartoons by Mark Davis at Mackerel

The publishers would like to thank the following sources for the use
of their photographs:
Page 32 (B) Fred Bavendam/Minden Pictures/FLPA
Page 42/43 (B) Michael Prince/CORBIS
Page 45 (CR) Warner Bros/Pictorial Press
Page 46/47 (FP) Amos Nachoum/CORBIS

All other images come from the Miles Kelly Archives, digital vision

www.mileskelly.net
info@mileskelly.net

Contents

Sharks swarm the seas

1 Sharks are meat-eating fish, and nearly all of them live in the sea. Every kind of shark is a meat-eater or carnivore. Many are active hunters and chase after their prey. Some lie in wait to grab victims. Others are scavengers, feasting on the dying and dead bodies of animals such as whales and seals.

▼ The sand tiger has all the typical shark features – beady eyes, nostrils for sensing scents, a wide mouth with sharp teeth, gill slits for underwater breathing, a powerful tail for swimming, fins for steering – and a huge appetite for many kinds of prey!

Every sea and ocean in the world has sharks — but there are very few in the coldest waters around Antarctica.

Some sharks are giants

2 **The biggest fish in the world is a type of shark called the whale shark.** It grows to 12 metres long, about the same as three family cars end-to-end. It can weigh over 12 tonnes, which is three times heavier than three family cars put together!

3 **Despite the whale shark's huge size, it mostly eats tiny prey.** It opens its enormous mouth, takes in a great gulp of water and squeezes it out through the gill slits on either side of its neck. Inside the gills, small animals such as shrimplike krill, little fish and baby squid are trapped and swallowed.

► Krill look like small shrimps and are usually 2 to 3 centimetres long. Millions of them, along with other small creatures, make up plankton.

4 **Whale sharks like cruising across the warm oceans, swimming up to 5000 kilometres in one year.** They wander far and wide, but tend to visit the same areas at certain times of year, when their food is plentiful.

▲ The whale shark swims with its mouth wide open to filter krill from the water. It sometimes swallows larger animals, such as penguins, smaller sharks and tuna fish.

5 **Whale sharks may sleep for months!** It's thought that they sink to the seabed and lie there, hardly moving, for several weeks each year. This could help them to save energy when food is scarce.

▶ Ripple patterns on basking sharks are caused by sunlight shining through the waves onto the shark.

6 **Basking sharks are huge, too.** They are the second-biggest of all fish, reaching 10 metres in length and 6 tonnes in weight. Like whale sharks, basking sharks filter small animals and bits of food from the sea.

7 **Some sharks like to eat stinking, rotting flesh!** The Greenland shark eats the meat from all kinds of dead bodies. These include whales, seals, dolphins, other sharks, squid and even drowned animals, such as reindeer.

▶ The Arctic water is very cold, so Greenland sharks can only swim slowly.

Sharks outlived dinosaurs!

8 The first sharks lived more than 350 million years ago. This was 120 million years before the dinosaurs appeared on Earth. Dinosaurs died out 65 million years ago but sharks survived. So sharks have ruled the seas for over twice as long as dinosaurs ruled the land!

9 Some prehistoric fish are called 'spiny sharks'. They looked like sharks with streamlined bodies and sharp spikes on their fins and bellies. Their real name is acanthodians, and they lived in lakes and rivers 400 to 250 million years ago.

MAKE MEGALODON'S MOUTH!

You will need:
black pen big cardboard box
large pieces of white card
scissors tape
1. Use a pen to draw a shark's mouth onto the box and cut it out.
2. Draw and cut out 20 teeth shapes.
3. Tape these inside the mouth. Draw on eyes. Now you can stare *Megalodon* in the face!

◄ Sharks' basic body shapes and behaviour have hardly changed since they first appeared. The shark *Hybodus* lived about 160 million years ago in the Jurassic period, during the age of dinosaurs.

10 Bits of shark have turned to stone!

Parts of sharks that died long ago have been preserved in rocks, as fossils. Most fossils are made of the hard parts, such as teeth and scales. These show the size of the shark and the kind of food it ate.

◄ *Megalodon* was probably similar in shape to the great white shark of today.

11 The biggest shark in history was probably *Megalodon*.

Its fossil teeth look like those of the great white shark, but they're twice as big. *Megalodon* could have been 15 or even 20 metres long – three times the size of today's great white. It lived about 20 to 2 million years ago and was one of the greatest hunters the animal world has ever known.

Super swimmers

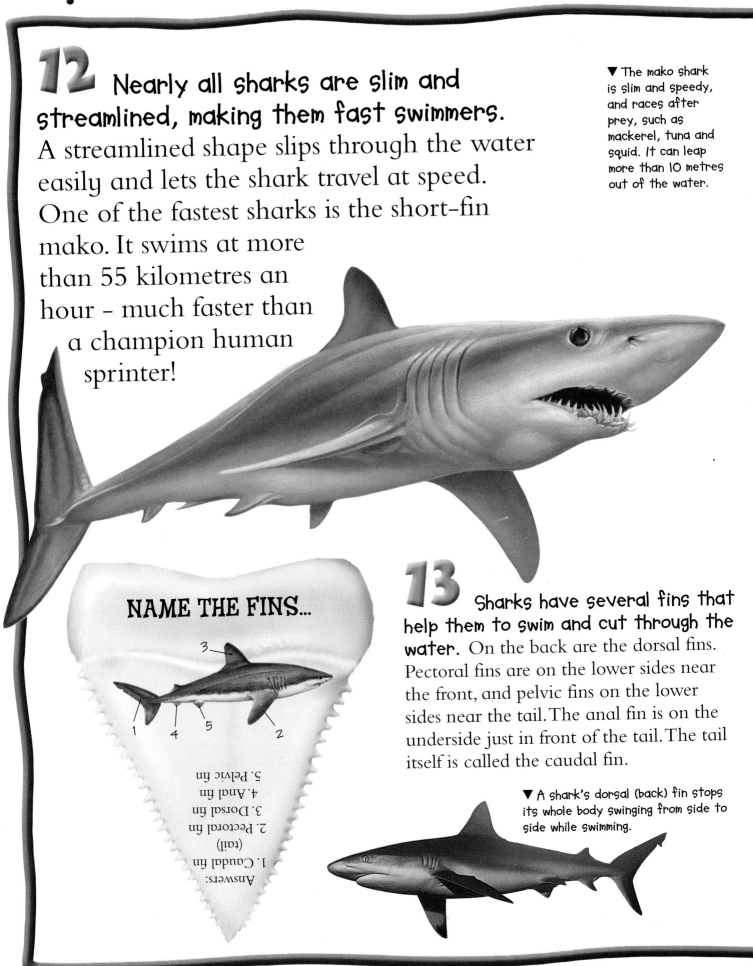

12 Nearly all sharks are slim and streamlined, making them fast swimmers. A streamlined shape slips through the water easily and lets the shark travel at speed. One of the fastest sharks is the short-fin mako. It swims at more than 55 kilometres an hour – much faster than a champion human sprinter!

▼ The mako shark is slim and speedy, and races after prey, such as mackerel, tuna and squid. It can leap more than 10 metres out of the water.

NAME THE FINS...

3
1 4 5 2

Answers:
1. Caudal fin (tail)
2. Pectoral fin
3. Dorsal fin
4. Anal fin
5. Pelvic fin

13 Sharks have several fins that help them to swim and cut through the water. On the back are the dorsal fins. Pectoral fins are on the lower sides near the front, and pelvic fins on the lower sides near the tail. The anal fin is on the underside just in front of the tail. The tail itself is called the caudal fin.

▼ A shark's dorsal (back) fin stops its whole body swinging from side to side while swimming.

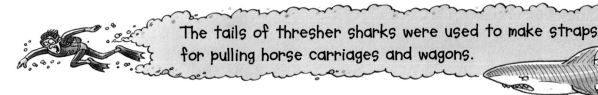
14 **Some sharks have tails longer than their bodies!** The common thresher shark is 6 metres long – and half of this is its tail. The thresher uses it to slap and bash smaller fish, so it can eat them.

▼ The thresher thrashes its tail from side to side to stun small fish before swallowing them.

15 **Shark tails have other uses, too.** Some sharks smack the water's surface with their tails to frighten their prey. Others swish away sand or mud on the seabed to reveal any hidden prey.

16 **Like other fish, sharks breathe underwater using their gills.** These are under the slits on either side of the head, and are filled with blood. Water flows in through the shark's mouth, over the gills and out through the slits. The gills take in oxygen from the water because sharks, like other animals, need oxygen to survive.

▶ A shark's gill chambers are in its neck region. Most have five gill slits on either side.

Gill rakers

Mouth

Gill slit

Gill filaments

Gill septum

17 **Most sharks must swim continuously, so that water flows over their gills and they can breathe.** Some can lie still and make the water flow over their gills by 'pumping' the muscles of their mouth and neck.

Sharks eat almost anything!

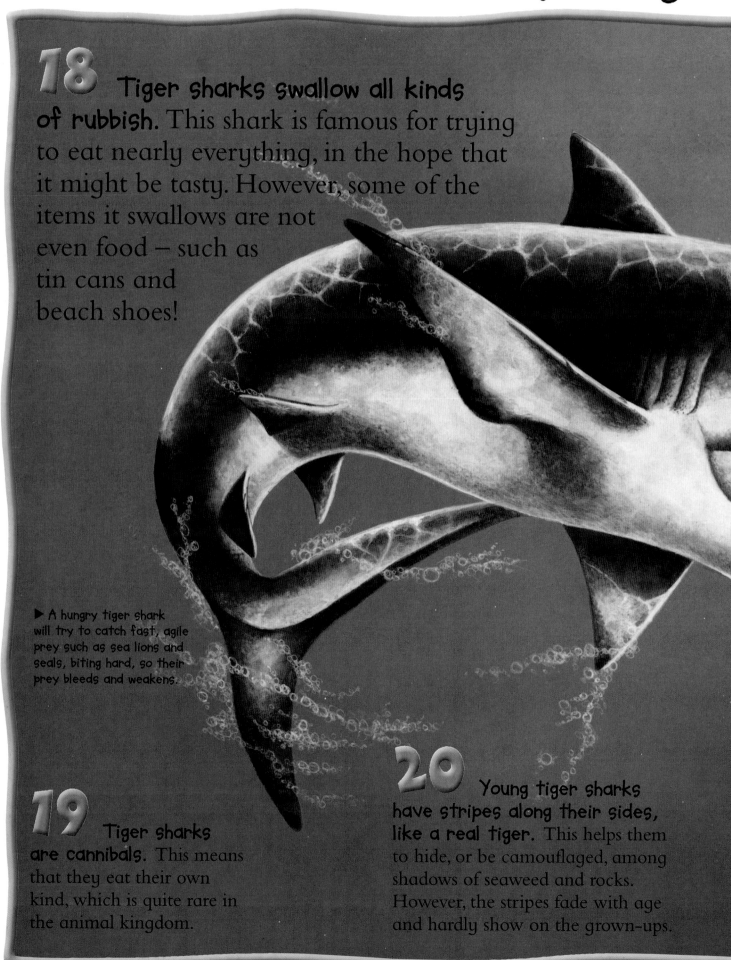

18 Tiger sharks swallow all kinds of rubbish. This shark is famous for trying to eat nearly everything, in the hope that it might be tasty. However, some of the items it swallows are not even food – such as tin cans and beach shoes!

▶ A hungry tiger shark will try to catch fast, agile prey such as sea lions and seals, biting hard, so their prey bleeds and weakens.

19 Tiger sharks are cannibals. This means that they eat their own kind, which is quite rare in the animal kingdom.

20 Young tiger sharks have stripes along their sides, like a real tiger. This helps them to hide, or be camouflaged, among shadows of seaweed and rocks. However, the stripes fade with age and hardly show on the grown-ups.

21 Tiger sharks swim right up to the beach! Most sharks stay away from the shore in case they get stranded and die. But tiger sharks come near to the shore, especially at night, to explore for food. They don't seem to mind swimming in water that's so shallow, it would hardly cover your knees. This can make it dangerous to go paddling!

I DON'T BELIEVE IT!
Tiger sharks have eaten all kinds of strange things — bottles, tools, car tyres, and in one case, a type of drum called a tom-tom!

22 Most sharks prefer just a few types of food. One kind of bullhead shark likes to eat only sea urchins. However, if it gets very hungry, it will try other foods.

23 Not all sharks have sharp, pointed teeth. The Port Jackson shark has wide, broad teeth, like rounded pebbles. It uses these to crush the hard body cases of its favourite food — shellfish.

Sharks have no bones!

▶ The main parts of the skeleton are the skull, the ribs, the long backbone or vertebral column, and the fin spines.

Skull

Supporting rods inside dorsal fin

Backbone or spine

Second dorsal fin

Supporting rods inside the tail

Ribs

Pectoral fin

Pelvic fin

Anal fin

24 A shark has a skeleton, like you do – but it has no bones! Its skeleton is made out of a substance called cartilage, or gristle. This is very strong and light, and also slightly bendy.

25 A shark's guts are about twice as long as its body. Swallowed food goes into the shark's stomach, then along the intestine. This has a part called a spiral valve, found in no other creatures except sharks and rays. It is shaped like a corkscrew and takes in nutrients from food.

26 Sharks have very tough skin covered with tiny, tooth-shaped points, called denticles. In the bramble shark some of the denticles are much larger, forming sharp thorns and prickles for protection.

Denticle

A shark's teeth are really much larger, stronger versions of its skin or scales.

27 Shark skin can be useful.

Through the ages it has been used by people as a strong material to make handbags, shoes, belts, cases, handle grips and even a special kind of sandpaper known as chagrin.

▲ Shark products such as bags and even vitamin pills have been made for centuries, but today many sharks are rare and need protecting.

28 Many sharks produce slime.

The slime made by the skin slides off easily and helps the shark to swim faster. New slime is always being made quickly by the skin to replace the slime that flows away. If a shark is trapped in a net, it thrashes about and tries to escape. This can damage the slime layer and cause cuts and sores on the skin.

WHICH BODY BITS ARE...

A. Inside a shark but not inside you?
B. Inside you but not inside a shark?
C. Inside you and a shark?

1. Stomach
2. Lungs
3. Spiral valve
4. Liver
5. Gills

Answers:
1. C 2. B
3. A 4. C
5. A

▲ The bramble shark is very 'thorny', studded with extra-large denticles. It is a slow swimmer and grows to 4 metres long.

Ultimate killer

29 The world's biggest predatory, or hunting, fish is the great white shark. In real life it is certainly large — at 6 metres in length and weighing more than one tonne. Great whites live around the world, mainly in warmer seas. They have a fearsome reputation.

▼ Great whites are curious about unfamiliar items in the sea. They often come very close to investigate anti-shark cages and the divers protected inside. This is partly because great whites are always on the lookout for food.

I DON'T BELIEVE IT!

The risk of being struck by lightning is 20 times greater than the risk of being attacked by a shark.

30 Great whites get hot! This is because they can make their bodies warmer than the surrounding water. This allows their muscles to work more quickly, so they can swim faster and more powerfully. It means the great white is partly 'warm-blooded' like you.

31 The great white has 50 or more teeth and each one is up to 6 centimetres long. The teeth are razor-sharp but slim, like blades, and they sometimes snap off. But new teeth are always growing just behind, ready to move forward and replace the snapped-off teeth.

32 The great white often attacks unseen from below. It surges up from the dark depths with tremendous power. It can smash into a big prey such as a seal or a dolphin, and lift it right out of the water as it takes its first bite.

33 Great whites let their victims bleed to death. They bite on their first charge then move off, leaving the victim with terrible wounds. When the injured prey is weak, the great white comes back to devour its meal.

34 The great white 'saws' lumps of food from its victim. Each tooth has tiny sharp points along its edges. As the shark starts to feed, it bites hard and then shakes its head from side to side. The teeth work like rows of small saws to slice off a mouthful.

Strange sharks

35 **Six-gill sharks have an extra pair of gills.** This may be the number that ancient sharks had long ago, before they developed into modern sharks. Six-gill sharks are up to 5 metres long and eat various foods, from shellfish to dead dolphins.

▶ Each tooth of the frilled shark has three needle-like points for grabbing soft-bodied prey.

I DON'T BELIEVE IT!

The smallest sharks could lie curled up in your hand. The dwarf lanternshark is just 20 centimetres long.

36 **Some sharks are frilly.** The frilled shark has six pairs of wavy gill slits. It looks more like an eel than a shark, with a slim body 2 metres in length, and long frilly fins. It is dark brown in colour, lives in very deep waters and eats squid and octopus.

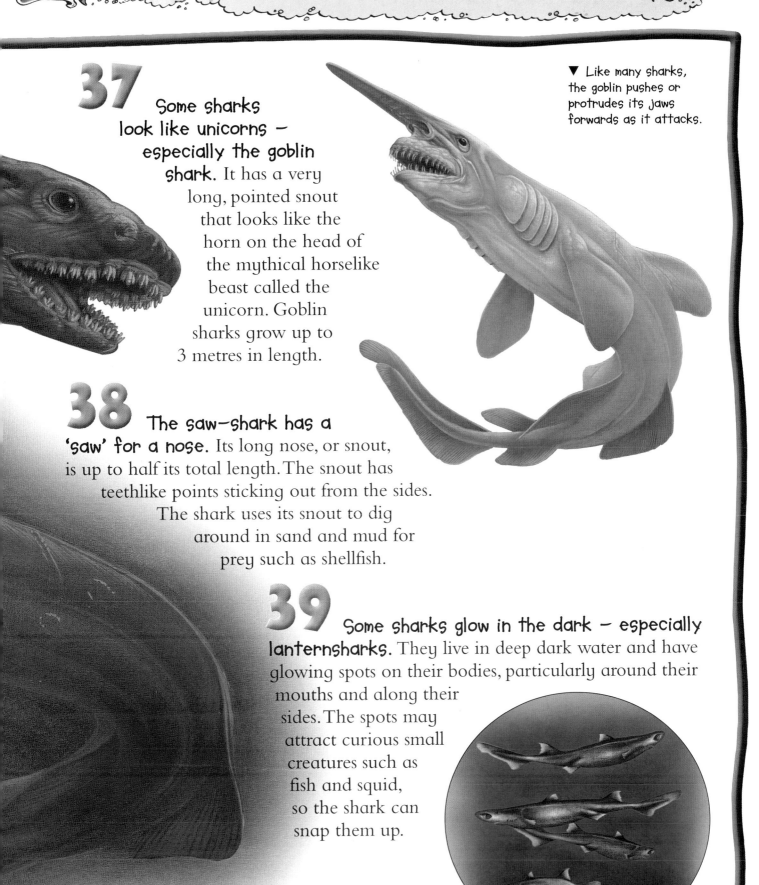

▼ Like many sharks, the goblin pushes or protrudes its jaws forwards as it attacks.

37

Some sharks look like unicorns – especially the goblin shark. It has a very long, pointed snout that looks like the horn on the head of the mythical horselike beast called the unicorn. Goblin sharks grow up to 3 metres in length.

38

The saw-shark has a 'saw' for a nose. Its long nose, or snout, is up to half its total length. The snout has teethlike points sticking out from the sides. The shark uses its snout to dig around in sand and mud for prey such as shellfish.

39

Some sharks glow in the dark – especially lanternsharks. They live in deep dark water and have glowing spots on their bodies, particularly around their mouths and along their sides. The spots may attract curious small creatures such as fish and squid, so the shark can snap them up.

▶ The lanternshark's tiny light-producing organs are called photophores.

Sharks are sensitive!

40 Most sharks have big eyes and can see well, especially in the dark. Many feed at night, or in deeper water where there's little light. This makes eyesight especially important to the shark so that it can spot its prey. Some sharks have eyes that glow in the dark, like a cat's.

▼ A porbeagle shark uses its keen eyesight to chase its favourite food – mackerel.

I DON'T BELIEVE IT!

The blind shark of Australia is not really blind! It can see very well. But when it's caught, it closes its eyes tightly, so it appears to have none.

41 Sharks have an amazing sense of smell. It is their best 'long-range' sense. From several kilometres away, they can detect blood or body fluids from a wounded animal. A shark 'sniffs' water into the nostrils on its snout, just like you sniff air into your nose.

42 Sharks often test-taste their food before eating. A shark often takes a small nibble of an unfamiliar food to check that it's suitable to eat. Some sharks have taste buds on their snouts, so they can detect the flavour of food by rubbing their noses on it.

43 Sharks can feel their way through narrow gaps in the dark, using the sense of touch on their skin. There is also a narrow strip along each side of a shark's body, called the lateral line. It can sense ripples and currents in the water from animals moving nearby.

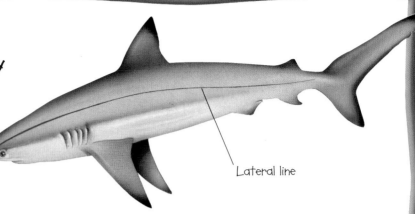

Lateral line

▲ The lateral line runs along the side of the body from head to tail base.

44 Sharks can hear divers breathing! They detect the sound of air bubbles coming from scuba-divers' mouths. But hearing is not the shark's best sense. Its ear openings are tiny, usually just behind the eyes.

▼ The electricity-sensing ampullae of Lorenzini show up as tiny holes over this great white's snout.

45 Sharks can detect electricity. As sea animals move, their muscles give off tiny pulses of electricity into the water. A shark has hundreds of tiny pits over its snout called ampullae of Lorenzini. These 'feel' the electric pulses. A shark can even detect prey buried out of sight in mud.

Hammers for heads

▲ The hammerhead's eyes, nostrils and electricity-sensing organs are at each end of the wing-shaped head.

46 **The hammerhead shark really does have a hammer-like head.** Experts suggest several reasons for this strange shape. One is that the head is shaped like the wings of a plane. As the shark swims, water flowing over its head helps to keep its front end lifted up, rather than nose-diving - just as wings keep a plane in the air.

47 **The hammer-shaped head may improve the shark's senses.** The nostrils are at each end of the 'hammer'. Smells drifting from the side reach one nostril well before the other. By swinging its head from side to side, the hammerhead can pinpoint the direction of a smell more quickly.

▼ Hammerheads often swim close to the seabed, searching for buried fish and shellfish.

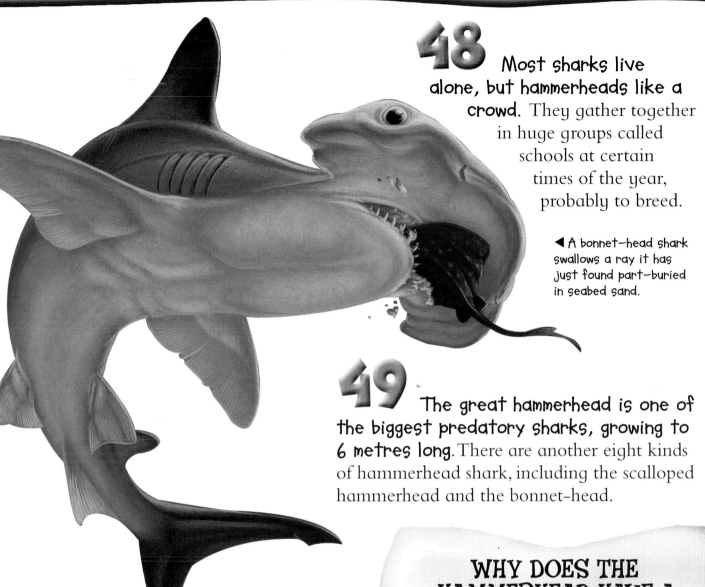

48 Most sharks live alone, but hammerheads like a crowd. They gather together in huge groups called schools at certain times of the year, probably to breed.

◀ A bonnet-head shark swallows a ray it has just found part-buried in seabed sand.

49 The great hammerhead is one of the biggest predatory sharks, growing to 6 metres long. There are another eight kinds of hammerhead shark, including the scalloped hammerhead and the bonnet-head.

50 Hammerheads are among the most dangerous sharks. They have been known to attack people, although their usual food includes fish, squid, crabs and shellfish. They eat stingrays too and don't seem to be affected by the painful sting. However, hammerheads are themselves eaten – by people. They are caught and cut up for their tasty meat and for the thick oil from their livers.

WHY DOES THE HAMMERHEAD HAVE A HAMMER-SHAPED HEAD?

1. To break apart rocks to get at prey behind them.
2. To help sense the direction of smells in the water.
3. To smash open windows in shipwrecks.

Answer:
2

Big mouth

51 The megamouth shark was discovered in 1976 near Hawaii in the Pacific Ocean. An American research ship hauled in its parachute-like anchor to find a strange shark tangled in it. Experts knew at once that this was a new type of shark, never described before.

52 The megamouth, as its name suggests, has a massive mouth more than 1.3 metres wide. Its soft, flabby body is about 5 metres long. In the summer when the megamouth has been feeding well, it can weigh more than one tonne.

53 Megamouths open their great mouths as they swim through shoals of small sea creatures, such as krill and young fish. The little prey get trapped inside the mouth and swallowed. The megamouth is not really an active hunter. It is a slow-swimming filter-feeder, like the whale shark and the basking shark.

54 Megamouths go up and down every day. They rise near the surface at dusk in order to feed during the night. At dawn they sink to deeper waters and spend the day in the dark, more than 200 metres down.

55 Megamouths are scattered around the world. They have been caught in all the tropical oceans, especially in the Western Pacific and Indian oceans. Only 20 or so have been found in the past 30 years. It may be that there have never been many megamouths in the world.

◄ The megamouth's huge jaws are right at the front of its body, not slung under the head as in most sharks.

The megamouth's mouth glows in the dark depths of the sea. Despite the vast size of the mouth, the teeth are tiny.

56 Scientists believe that there may be more types of shark as yet undiscovered. Sometimes the badly-rotted bodies of strange sharks are washed up onto beaches. But the remains are often too decayed to be identified.

The loose skin and floppy fins show that the megamouth is a slow swimmer.

Swimming with sharks

▼ This great white shark is about to take a bite out of a piece of meat dangled from a boat. Although it's not hunting, you can see how it lifts its snout up high and thrusts its teeth forward to attack.

57 Some small types of shark are fairly safe and people can swim near them with care. In some tourist areas, people can even feed sharks. The sharks seem to become trained to accept food from divers.

58 The cookie-cutter shark is only 50 centimetres long, with a large mouth and big, sharp teeth. This shark attacks fish much larger than itself, biting out small patches of skin and flesh, before racing away. Its victim is left with a neat round hole on its body – ouch!

59 Some sharks get so used to accepting food from people that they get out of the habit of hunting. When the people are no longer around, the shark starts to starve.

60 Feeding and touching sharks is now banned in some places. Sometimes a shark snatches and swallows the food while it's still in a bag or net. This could give the shark bad stomach-ache, or even kill it. Also, touching sharks and other fish can damage their delicate skin, scales and layers of body slime. Finally, using meat to feed small, harmless sharks could attract bigger, dangerous ones.

Which of these sharks are not usually dangerous to people?
1. White-tip reef shark
2. Great white
3. Nurse shark
4. Thresher
5. Tiger shark

Answers: 1 3 4

29

Shark cousins

61 Sharks have many close relations who, like themselves, have a skeleton made of cartilage rather than bone. Other kinds of cartilaginous fish include skates and rays, and the deep-water ratfish, or chimaera.

62 Skates and rays are flat fish, but not flatfish. True flatfish, such as plaice, have bony skeletons and lie on their left or right side. Skates and rays have very wide bodies with flattened upper and lower surfaces, and a long narrow tail.

▲ Chimaeras are also called ratfish after their long, tapering tails. Most are about one metre long.

63 A ray or skate 'flies' through the water. The sides of its body extend out like wings. The 'wings' push the water backwards, and so the ray or skate swims forwards. Unlike sharks and other fish, the ray's tail is seldom used for swimming.

► The huge manta ray has fleshy side flaps or 'horns' on its head that guide water into its mouth. It is shown here with a smaller and more common type of ray, the spotted eagle ray.

Spotted eagle ray

64

The biggest rays are mantas. They measure up to 7 metres across and weigh nearly 2 tonnes. Manta rays have huge mouths and feed like whale sharks by filtering small creatures from the water. Despite their great size, mantas can leap clear of the surface and crash back with a tremendous splash.

Manta ray

65

Stingrays have sharp spines on their long tails. They use them like a daggers to jab poison into enemies or victims. Some stingrays live in lakes and rivers.

66

Sawfish are different from saw—sharks. A sawfish is shaped like a shark, but is a type of ray with a long snout edged by pointed teeth. You can tell the difference between them because a sawfish has gill slits on the bottom of its body, rather than on the side.

THE 'FLYING' RAY

You will need:
scissors stiff paper coloured pens
sticky tape drinking straw
modelling clay

1. Cut out a ray shape from paper.
2. Colour it brightly. Fold it along the middle so the 'wings' angle upwards. Stick the straw along the underside, so part sticks out as a 'tail'. Add a blob of modelling clay to one end.
3. Launch your 'flying ray' into the air. Adjust the tail weight until it glides smoothly.

Sharks need partners

▼ A blue shark heads towards its traditional breeding area in a shallow part of the ocean near the coast to search for a mate.

67 Female sharks need male sharks of the same breed to produce young. When a male and a female get together, they mate. Then the female can produce offspring. Some types of shark lay eggs, while others give birth to live young.

▼ Hammerheads swim slowly in huge shoals at breeding time.

68 Some sharks gather in large groups, or shoals, to breed. Hammerheads come together in hundreds or even thousands, so the females and males can choose partners for mating. Bonnet-heads, nurse and dogfish sharks also form breeding shoals.

▶ Male white-tip reef sharks rest in the shallows, waiting for scents called pheromones to drift through the water, which tell them that females are nearby.

69 Sharks have a complicated way of getting together, known as courtship. They give off scents or 'perfumes' into the water to attract a partner. Then the two rub one another, wind their bodies around each other, and maybe even bite the other! The male may hold the female using his claspers, which are two long parts on his underside.

70 Some sharks don't breed very often. This can cause problems, especially when people catch too many of them. The sharks cannot breed fast enough to keep up their numbers, and they become rare and endangered.

Eggs and baby sharks

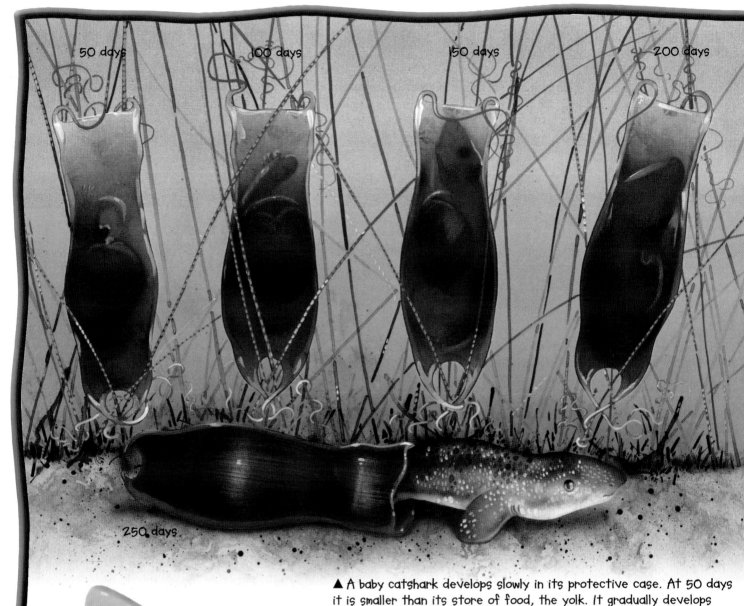

50 days   100 days   150 days   200 days

250 days

▲ A baby catshark develops slowly in its protective case. At 50 days it is smaller than its store of food, the yolk. It gradually develops and finally hatches eight months later.

71 **Some mother sharks lay eggs.** Each egg has a strong case with a developing baby shark, called an embryo, inside. The case has long threads, which stick to seaweed or rocks. Look out for empty egg cases on beaches. They are known as 'mermaids' purses'.

I DON'T BELIEVE IT!

As the young of the sand tiger shark develop inside their mother, the bigger ones feed on the smaller ones.

In most kinds of sharks, females have thick skin to protect against the bites of males during courtship.

72 **Some mother sharks do not lay eggs, but give birth to baby sharks, which are known as pups.** The hammerhead and the basking shark do this. The pups have to look after themselves straight away. Shark parents do not care for their young.

▲ A lanternshark baby, or pup, still attached to its yolk, which continues to nourish its growth.

73 **Some sharks have hundreds of babies at once!** The whale shark may give birth to as many as 300 pups, each about 60 centimetres long.

74 **Sadly, most young sharks die.** The mothers lay eggs or give birth in sheltered places such as bays, inlets and reefs, where there are plenty of places to hide. But the young sharks are easy prey for hunters such as dolphins, barracudas, sea lions – and other sharks.

▼ The egg cases of the Port Jackson shark are spiral-shaped. The mother picks up each egg in her mouth and wedges it into a safe place such as under a rock.

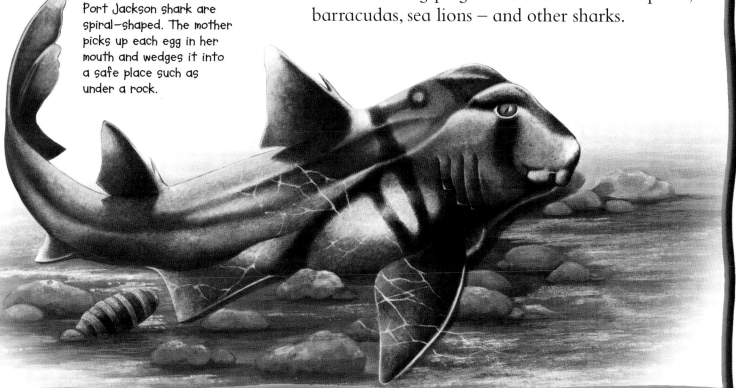

Sharks can 'disappear'

75 **Some sharks blend into their surroundings so well that they are hardly noticed.** This is called camouflage. The wobbegong has a lumpy body with blotches and frills that look just like rocks and seaweed. It waits for a fish to swim past, then opens its huge mouth to grab the victim.

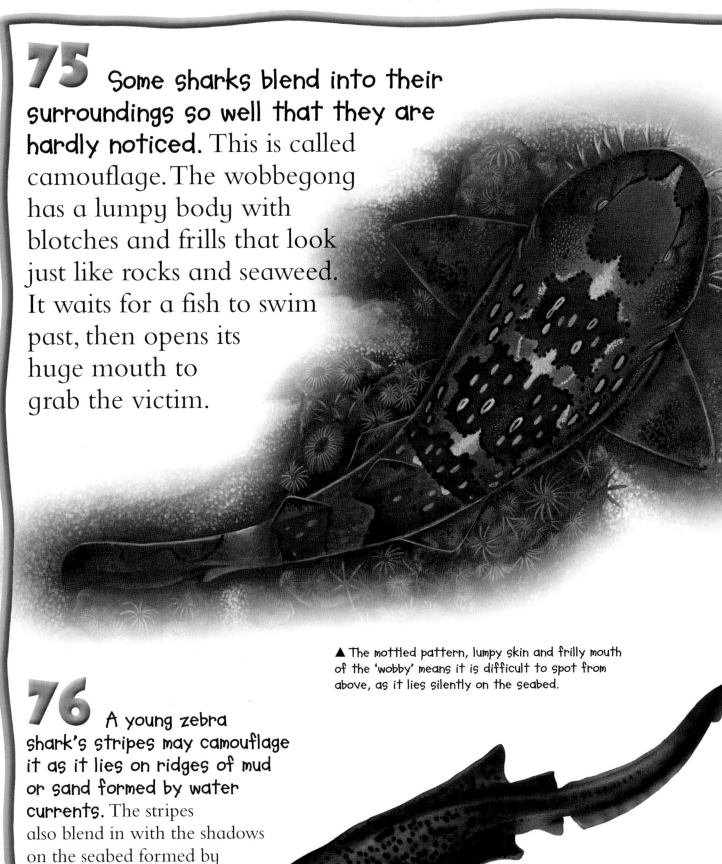

▲ The mottled pattern, lumpy skin and frilly mouth of the 'wobby' means it is difficult to spot from above, as it lies silently on the seabed.

76 **A young zebra shark's stripes may camouflage it as it lies on ridges of mud or sand formed by water currents.** The stripes also blend in with the shadows on the seabed formed by ripples on the surface above. As the shark grows, its stripes split into spots.

◄ This adult zebra shark's spots were once connected to form stripes.

77

Angel sharks have wide, flat bodies the same colour as sand. They blend perfectly into the sandy seabed as they lie in wait for prey. They are called 'angel' sharks because their fins spread wide like an angel's wings.

▶ The flattened body of the angel shark looks like a low lump in the sandy seabed.

78

Even in the open ocean, sharks can be hard to spot. This is because of the way they are coloured, known as countershading. The shark's back is darker while its underside is lighter. Seen from above the dark back blends in with the gloom of deeper water below. Seen from below the pale belly merges with the brighter water's surface and sky above.

▼ A side view of this silvertip shark shows countershading — darker back, lighter underside.

WHICH SHARKS LIVE WHERE?

Pair up these sharks and the habitats in which live.
1. Blue shark — light blue above, mainly white below
2. Wobbegong — green and brown blotches, lumps and frills
3. Spotted dogfish — dark blotches on light body
Habitats:
A. Sandy seabed
B. Open ocean
C. Rocks and weeds

Answers:
1 B
2 C 3 A

Shark friends

▼ Cleaner wrasse gather around the mouth and gill slits of this white-tip reef shark.

79 **Some fish enter a shark's mouth — and live!** These small, brightly coloured fish are called cleaner wrasse. The shark allows them to nibble off bits of skin, scales and pests such as sea leeches and barnacles, from its body, gills, mouth and teeth. The shark gets tidied up and has its teeth cleaned, and the cleaner fish have a good meal. A helpful relationship like this between two species of animal is called 'symbiosis'.

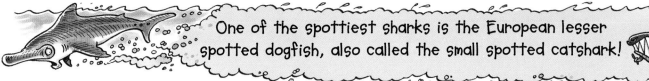
80

Some fish like to swim along very near to sharks. They are called pilotfish and often cluster just below and in front of the shark's mouth. They may feel safe from large predators that might eat them. They could be waiting for bits of food falling from the shark's mouth. Or they may be saving energy by swimming in the shark's slipstream – the swirls and currents made by its movement.

81

Some fish attach themselves to sharks and travel with them through the ocean. Remoras or sharksuckers have a ridged sucker on their heads. This clamps to the underside of a large shark (or other big sea creature). Using this, the remora saves energy by getting a free ride, and it can let go to feed on scraps from the shark's meal.

TRUE OR FALSE?

1. Fish that enter a shark's mouth are always eaten.
2. Remoras eat the scraps of food that sharks leave behind.
3. A helpful relationship between two different species of animal is called 'symbiosis'.

Answers:
1 False.
2 True. 3 True.

▼ This remora (below) has just detached from a bull shark, showing its sucker-topped head.

Sharks on the move

82 There are about 330 kinds of sharks, but only a few leave the salty water of the sea and swim into the fresh water of rivers. One is the bull shark, which travels hundreds of kilometres up rivers, especially in South America. It has attacked people fishing, washing or boating in lakes.

83 The most common sharks are blue sharks, which are found in almost every part of every ocean except the icy polar seas. In the Atlantic Ocean, they travel from the Caribbean to Western Europe, down to Africa, and back to the Caribbean – 6000 kilometres in one year!

84 Some sharks live in small areas and rarely stray outside them. One is the Galapagos shark, which swims around a few small groups of mid-ocean islands in the tropics.

▼ Not all sharks travel far afield. The Galapagos shark stays close to home, swimming only in one small area.

▶ One of the few sharks that regularly moves out of water is the epaulette shark. It drags itself between rock pools using its strong pectoral fins.

All epaulette sharks have a large black ocellus (an eye-like spot) above the pectoral fin

Large pectoral fins allow the epaulette shark to travel along the seabed

85 Epaulette sharks can leave the water and move over dry land. They can drag themselves along the seashore from one rock pool to the next by using their strong pectoral fins like 'arms'.

86 Sharks may have a built-in compass. People use magnetic compasses to find their way across the seas or remote lands. The compass detects the natural magnetism of the Earth and points north-south. Sharks may be able to detect the Earth's magnetism too, using tiny parts of their bodies. Other animals can do this too, such as certain birds and turtles. This could help sharks find their way across oceans.

I DON'T BELIEVE IT!

Most submarines can't dive beyond 500 metres, but the Portuguese shark can swim over 3500 metres below the surface.

Science and sharks

87 Scientists study sharks around the world – especially how they live, behave and travel. Small radio-transmitter trackers can be attached to big sharks and the radio signals show where the shark roams. Smaller sharks have little plastic tags with letters and numbers attached to their fins. If the shark is caught again, its code can be traced.

▲ This dogfish shark has a plastic tag fixed to its dorsal fin, so scientists can record its travels.

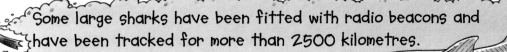
88 **Sharks show us problems in the oceans.** In some areas, sharks have disappeared for no obvious reason. This might suggest chemicals and pollution in the water, which upset the balance of nature. The chemicals could affect the sharks themselves, making them feel unwell so that they travel away. Or the pollution could affect the sharks' prey, such as small fish. Then the sharks have to hunt elsewhere for food.

▼ Huge aquariums let us watch the fascinating underwater world of sharks and other fish.

89 **Some sharks can live in captivity.** They are very popular with visitors to sea-life centres and aquariums. People love to get up close to sharks and see their teeth, eyes, fins, and their grace and power as they swim. The captured animals can also help us to learn more about the species and how to protect them and their natural habitats.

90 **Sharks may help us to find new medicines.** Sharks seem to suffer from diseases and infections quite rarely compared to other animals. Scientists are examining their body parts, blood and the natural chemicals they produce in order to make better medical drugs for humans.

Shark attacks

▲ From below, a surfboard looks similar to a seal or a turtle, which may be the reason why large hunting sharks sometimes attack surfers.

91 The most dangerous sharks include the great white, tiger and bull sharks. However, a shark that attacks a person might not be properly identified. Attacks happen very quickly and the shark is soon gone. Some attacks blamed on great whites might well have been made by bull sharks instead.

▶ Great whites do sometimes attack humans, but their favourite foods are fish, seals and sealions.

92 Areas of the world known for shark attacks include the east coast of North America, the west coast of Africa and around Southeast Asia and Australia. This is partly because these places are popular with swimmers and surfers.

93 Most shark attacks are not fatal. A shark may 'test-bite' a person and realize that this is not its usual prey. The victim may be injured, but not killed.

◀ Even quite large sharks are themselves hunted, by the huge elephant seal, which can weigh up to 5 tonnes.

94 Sharks do not attack people because they hate us. They are simply hungry and looking for a meal. They may sometimes mistake humans for their usual prey, such as sea lions.

95 The dangers of shark attacks can be reduced in many ways. Examples include shark barriers or nets around the beach, patrols by boats and planes, lookout towers, and only swimming in protected areas between flags.

▶ Movies about sharks often make them seem more eager to attack than in reality. The 1999 film *Deep Blue Sea* features blood-thirsty ultra-intelligent sharks.

I DON'T BELIEVE IT!

Each year there are less than ten fatal shark attacks — ten times less than the number of people killed by falling coconuts!

96 Sharks are not the most dangerous animals, by a long way! Each year, many more people are killed by poisonous snakes, tigers, elephants, hippos and crocodiles. Some tiny animals are much more lethal. Mosquitoes spread the disease malaria, which kills more than one million people every year.

Save our sharks

97 Some sharks have become very rare. They include the most feared of all, the great white. There are many reasons – hunting by people who think that all sharks are dangerous, sports angling where people use rods and lines to hook sharks, pollution, catching sharks for people to eat, and catching sharks by accident in nets meant for other fish such as tuna.

98 Sharks are made into many foods, including shark's-fin soup. Many other shark parts are eaten by people around the world, including the flesh as shark steaks, and the liver and other body parts in various oils, cosmetics and health foods. Sometimes, it's not obvious because names are changed. Meat from the small dogfish shark may be sold as 'rock salmon' or 'rock cod'.

▲ By getting very close to sharks, and studying their detailed behaviour, experts can help the conservation effort.

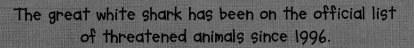

The great white shark has been on the official list of threatened animals since 1996.

99 Live sharks can be worth more than dead ones. People pay to see sharks in their natural habitats, viewing from glass-bottomed boats or underwater tunnels. In ecotourism, people experience nature without damaging it, and profits are used to help animals, plants and their habitats.

QUIZ

Put these sharks in order of size, starting with the smallest to the biggest:
A. Great white
B. Lesser spotted dogfish
C. Nurse shark
D. Frilled shark

100 Some sharks need our help, or they will die out forever. One of the best ways is to set aside huge areas of sea and coast as marine nature reserves or sanctuaries. Here all the animals can be protected from the most dangerous creature on Earth – the human.

Answers:
1.B 2.D
3.C 4.A

Index